Oracle Cards

Guidebook

Toni Carmine Salerno

Universal Wisdom
Oracle Cards

Published by Just Imagine Arthouse
80 Glen Tower Drive
Glen Waverley. Victoria. Australia 3150
Phone: 61 3 9574 7776   Fax: 61 3 9574 7772
E-mail: toni@justimagine-arthouse.com

Artwork from original paintings by...	Toni Carmine Salerno
Guidebook and messages...	Toni Carmine Salerno
Graphic design and artistic direction...	Aspen Michael Taylor
Editing...	Tanya Graham

ISBN: 0- 9579149-1-1

Dedicated to

World Peace

Earth in Transition

Our world is undergoing a huge transformation. It is my belief that the developments now unfolding will eventually lead to a time of peace. The turbulent times we currently face are the gateway through which humanity will enter the portal of love. We are at the crossroads, reconsidering our priorities and assessing our beliefs.

As the world is plunged deeper into chaos by global problems, we shall come to realise that in order to have peace in our world, we must let go of fear and judgement and embrace love and compassion.

We are energetically connected to one another and to our planet and therefore, what affects one, affects all. If there is but one homeless person upon this Earth or one who is hungry, then it is up to all of us to help shelter and feed that person.

As each new day unfolds, more of us are beginning to discover our spirit and awaken to our inner power. Humanity is in search of peace, greater meaning, and truth. Through this awakening we will come to realise what is perhaps the greatest of all spiritual truths and that is, that energetically, all is inextricably linked.

Creation exists as a whole; there is no separation. Many are already aware of this truth and their love and wisdom is of great assistance to our Earth at this time.

Even if you look at all that is happening from a purely physical perspective, it is obvious that the state of the world is far from ideal. Fear and uncertainty have to some degree crept into all our lives. However, the current circumstances offer us the opportunity to think about the kind of world we wish to live in and the kind of world we wish to leave for our children.

Perhaps it is only through necessity that we have started to look at all the injustice that exists. However, behind this physical necessity lies a deeper spiritual purpose, which is driving the current sequence of events.

We have moved into the Age of Aquarius, which brings with it a desire for peace and healing. In order to achieve this peace and healing, all humanity's fears, prejudices and hatreds must be expressed, so that they may be healed. Healing cannot occur when all these feelings and emotions remain buried in people's hearts. Through these turbulent times shall emerge a greater understanding of life. Hopefully we will look back at this time and see the current events as a blessing.

It is barely the start of the new millennium and already we are right in the thick of it, not sure what the present or the future holds. There is valid reason for fear, however, there is even greater reason for hope. For through the present darkness we shall come to see the light. Trust, make love your focus and let go of fear.

The Twentieth Century was a time of incredible change. Enormous advancements were made in science, technology and medicine. One of the legacies the Twentieth Century has left us, is the possibility of instant communication across the globe and instant access to vast volumes of information. We are witness to much of what goes on in the world and we have access to a wide range of perspectives on any issue.

This ability to communicate and share ideas and information is an opportunity for us to witness the injustices of the world and to break down the walls of prejudice and ignorance, which can no longer be ignored.

We shall come to accept that there is no one single truth in the world. The truth is different for each of us. All we can do is honour our own truth, while respecting the views and truths of others. All that matters is that we cause no harm to the Earth or to any other living thing.

The events of September 11, 2001 have impacted on all our lives. Through the darkness, much has come to light. Aware of the divisions that exist among us, the events unfolding show us that it is no longer reasonable to hold on to stubborn and righteous views and delude ourselves that our own views are necessarily 'right'. We are being forced to look at our lives and beliefs from a broader perspective and accept that others may have completely different views and beliefs to our own.

This does not necessarily mean that we should change what we believe, but perhaps we could all be a bit more flexible in our views and show greater tolerance and compassion for the views and beliefs of others.

If we look at the history of our planet and the history of our lives on a spiritual level, it can all be traced back to two things — love and fear. The way we react to the events in our lives ultimately depends on whether we are motivated by love or fear.

We cannot control the course of our lives, however we have the power to choose how we react to the events that unfold. We can choose to embrace love or fear and this choice determines what our experience will be.

This card set has been designed to assist you in this time of transition. It offers spiritual guidance, to help you reflect upon that which your heart desires, and to help you to truly love yourself, for in doing so, you will transform not only your own life but also our world.

Having been raised in a society based on fear, we often disregard or suppress what we truly feel in our hearts and allow the rational mind or 'ego'

*to control our lives. We have little understanding
of our feelings and little faith in spirit.*

*How many decisions have you made that were
truly based on your heart's desire? How often have
you settled for second best simply because you did
not believe you deserved any better? Many a truly
heartfelt wish or beautiful idea has been crushed
by the negative voice of fear. Society's disapproval
has cast shadows on the dreams of many.*

*These cards are not here to predict the future,
they are here to encourage you to embrace the creative
and healing power of love inside you. They
encourage you to live your dream and be the
wondrous beauty that you truly are. I offer them to
you in the hope that they may help to guide and
empower you to lead a wonderful life. They offer
personal guidance, yet remember that we each mirror
a piece of the tapestry that is this world; and therefore,
these cards relate also to our world as a whole.*

Love

The magical power of love may be beyond our understanding, yet we all seek love and the happiness it brings. Love has the power to transform and change our lives; all it requires is faith, for faith gives love power.

Yet so often, faith gives in to fear. Something in us believes that if we are fearful, we will have a better chance of avoiding the things that 'go wrong' in life. However, when fear becomes our driving force, our decisions are made not from truth but from a false and distorted sense of reality.

Fear is a belief system which excludes love and in doing so excludes any trust in the Divine. If we believe that we live in a world that is purely physical, it is difficult for us to have faith and trust in anything other than human logic. We are restricted by what we think is possible, rather than soaring to new heights in the knowledge that possibility is infinite.

If you believe that everything in life has a spirit and that love is its driving force, then it is easier for you to live to your full potential and to live in accordance with the wishes of your soul. Your feelings are the gateway to an unlimited universe, where everything is possible and creation is endless. Believe creation to be abundant, follow your heart and you will be fulfilled.

Love works in mysterious ways. At times it requires us to surrender our will and step into the unknown. Ironically, fear can do the opposite; it gives us the illusion that we are in control. Although we feel afraid, we feel we are in the driver's seat. This strange sense of security that fear can give us will sooner or later be shattered. At some point we all come to realise that life is never totally under our control. In the words of John Lennon, "life is what happens to you while you're busy making other plans".

And so it is that while we are focused on what we think we want to do, life seems to have an agenda all of its own. Our plans and all the energy we put into them can sometimes take a dramatic turn.

Remember, when you pass from this world you take nothing with you but your soul and the memories it holds. Your spirit is the most important thing in your life, for it holds your highest truth. Nurture your spirit through love.

Observe your thoughts. Each time you catch yourself running a fearful thought, consciously replace it with a positive and loving one. Love yourself. Love is the only truth you will ever need. Love is the fabric of life, indestructible and eternal.

The Oracle Cards

The meanings of these oracle cards lie equally in the messages and the images. The messages appear in the following pages, while the images hold encoded messages, energetically, through their vibration. There is no single meaning to each card. It may be different for each of us, for the images contain many layers of meaning. Both the messages and the paintings in this deck have been created intuitively, that is, without prior thought or planning. All my work is created in this way as this process leaves no room for the limitations of the intellect to flow through to my work. The same thing happens when you choose a card. You are guided by your soul to pick the card that is most appropriate for you at that time. A higher vibration flows through when you work in unison with the universal spirit of life.

In Love and Light,
Toni Carmine Salerno

How to Use these Cards

One Card Reading

Think of a question and hold it in your mind, then pick a card at random. Or, if you can't think of a question, simply pick a card and something that desires attention will present itself.

Either way, the cards are chosen by your soul or guiding angel to deliver a message which can be of assistance to you today. Their primary purpose is not to predict the future but to mirror the present. They are here to encourage you and to help you heal yourself.

The image on each card holds an energetic message, which works through vibration and the subconscious mind, while the guidebook holds information, which can be absorbed both consciously and subconsciously. The cards may confirm something for you or present you with a new issue that relates to your present circumstances. Either way, they are designed to encourage you along life's journey and shed light on anything that is of importance.

Remember that often the current issues and situations in our life stem from our past. We are often presented with a similar, challenging situation over and over again. It may seem that you've been there and done that, yet here you are again faced with the same situation. If this is the case, it usually means that there are unresolved issues, which stem from your past. The same issues appear in your life, often only in different guises, to give you a fresh opportunity to address and heal them. We keep experiencing these similar situations because there is something still to be learnt from them and this prevents us from moving on to other experiences.

So, if you pick a card with a specific question in mind and find that you are puzzled by the answer, remember that the card may actually be presenting you with an underlying issue or cause that needs to be addressed. Allow yourself time and do not take it all too seriously. Life is a game and it helps to laugh every once in a while.

Four Card Reading

You can use the four card reading to help you find the answer to a specific question your have in mind or simply pick the cards and see what comes up.

1. *To begin, pick the first card and place it face up. This card represents the present situation.*

2. *Pick the second card and place it to the left of the first one. This card reveals how the present issue ties in with your past. It may either reveal that you have worked through a past issue, which has helped create the present situation, or, that this past issue is something that needs to be kept in mind and addressed in order for you to move forward.*

3. *Pick your third and fourth cards and place them to the right of the first card. These two cards give you an insight into two possible outcomes that relate to the present issue in your life. You have a choice on how you deal with this issue.*

No matter what you are faced with you always have a choice in how you react to and deal with things. You can choose to work through this issue with love or you can react to it through fear. Love is always where your truth is. Remember, that it is in the present that the seeds of your future are sown. Your future experience depends on the thoughts and intentions you plant now and on the work you are willing to do on yourself today.

About the Artist

Toni Carmine Salerno is a self-taught artist, born of Italian parents on 20 October 1954. He lives and works from his home-studio in Melbourne, Australia. While he has been painting and writing poetry since eleven years of age, it was not until around 1994 that he decided to fully embrace what has always been his passion in life. He has been writing and painting full-time ever since. An artistic journey steeped in spirituality and mysticism has been at times a hard and lonely road, with doubts, fears and insecurities to face in the process. It is the path of The Mystic, where the next step forward is never quite clear.

Toni's art is forever evolving and changing, however the mystical and dreamlike quality of his work always remains. His work ranges from abstract/ethereal to figurative/realism. Spirit and matter merge in his work. The Sky and Sun melt into the Earth, trees encase the Moon and the Sea becomes an ocean of light. A feminine spirit emerges from within the heart of a flower or she lies naked and dreaming upon the ocean. Love radiates from his work to touch a place deep inside the observer.

Having no desire to follow trends, he is purely guided by intuition and feeling. He is a deeply spiritual person, who believes that love is the essential quality that underpins our lives and all of creation. He does not belong to any group and follows no particular doctrine, believing that being religious is not necessarily the same thing as being spiritual. In Toni's words, "Spirituality is the life force within all things. A blade of grass holds the same spiritual energy that we all do. We are no more and no less, for all in creation is one".

Apart from the occasional use of models as inspiration for some paintings, Toni's work is intuitive; rarely does he hold a preconceived idea of what he will write or paint.

One of the artist's main passions is to assist others to connect with their own creativity. "By getting in touch with what you are feeling and letting go of preconceived ideas, you are able to connect to the endless source of creative energy within you". This is Toni's message to all those who attend his intuitive art and writing workshops.

For Toni, art and creativity are expressions of the soul. Art exists in everyone; it deserves encouragement and requires nurturing. Art should not be judged, but seen for what it is. Art is healing, inspiration and therapy for the soul. We each have a story to tell, we each have something unique to share. Art offers us the opportunity to express life in ways that transcend our physical limitations and the limitations of a three-dimensional mind. Creativity, like spirit is multi-dimensional and endless.

Some of Toni's other passions include Reiki and Meditation, which he includes in his workshops. He has a strong interest in works by ancient philosophers and poets, especially those of the Roman poet, Virgil and the fourteenth century Florentine poet, Dante.

He is the author of two books, "Jewels Within a Teardrop" and "Just Imagine" as well as the author of "Universal Love – Healing Oracle Cards".

His work is now being reproduced and distributed in many parts of the world including Europe, Britain and America.

For Information

*Universal Wisdom — Oracle Cards are the
sequel to Universal Love — Healing Oracle,
which also comprises of forty-five cards and a
guidebook.*

*For information regarding previous publications
or to receive a catalogue of available art prints
and greeting cards featuring the artist's work
please contact...*

Just Imagine Arthouse
80 Glen Tower Drive
Glen Waverley, Victoria, 3150
Australia

E-mail: info@justimagine-arthouse.com

Toni Carmine Salerno's
artwork is also on the Internet at:
www.justimagine-arthouse.com

Contents

❧ *Abundance* ❧

Abundance is the natural state of the Universe and of all creation. Abundance exists all around you and your life can be filled with abundance provided you feel it first inside your heart and mind. Allow yourself to give and receive freely without fear or apprehension and in doing so, you will create an endless flow of abundance in your life.

Affirmation

I have abundance in my life.
I am abundant on all levels.
I have abundance of health,
Wealth, joy, love and happiness.
I share my abundance with others,
Knowing I will never be without.
I give thanks for the many blessings
I receive each day.
My world and the Universe are full of abundance.

❧ Acceptance ❧

Everything happens for a reason; even though the reason may often be unclear to us. Trust in this and accept life as it unfolds, living fully within each moment. Allow love into your heart. The purpose of your life is to discover and accept your own truth. Be yourself — not the personality you project to others, but the 'real you'. Express and radiate the beauty that exists at the core of your being.

Allow yourself to be vulnerable and share your insecurities, concerns and fears. Share all that you hold in your heart and know that in doing so, you are a gift to others, for you show them that it is alright to express how they feel also.

Self-acceptance enables you to express your truth and honour the spirit of your life.

This card also relates to a gift of some kind that is coming your way in the near future. Accept it with open arms and an open heart. It is a gift from the Universe. Through acceptance you can start to truly love yourself and embrace all of who you are.

Acceptance is the path to love; it connects mind and body with spirit. Stop struggling with life and accept all that you are. Through this you will come to see, feel and be all the beauty that you truly are.

Affirmation

I accept who I am with love.
I choose to see the beauty in my life.
My life is part of the Divine Plan.
My life is sacred.
I surrender all struggle to the infinite light
of my spirit.
I am eternal.
I am free.

❧ *Amethyst Wings* ❧

A heart transforms to amethyst,
Grows wings and sets flight towards the moon.

The amethyst angel has appeared in your reading today to bless you and let you know that the turmoil you are currently experiencing is there to clear the way for a positive transformation.

Amethyst is a crystal that helps transform and transmute the energies that no longer serve us. Your soul has yearned for this transformation and has ignited the flame. Your heart yearns for you to be happy and free you from inner turmoil and conflict. What is about to be released and transformed is anger and fear which have been secretly stored within the recesses of your heart, so well so, that you may hardly be aware that you have them.

Transformation is in essence change which we instinctively resist. We often have no clear idea what change will bring. Part of us, especially the mind, feels secure in what is familiar and wants to hang on to things just the way they are.

Meanwhile, our heart yearns for this transformation, for it desires greater freedom. Your spirit can see the bigger picture of your life and has sown the seeds of change. The message for you today is go with the flow. Struggle not — allow the transformation. Surrender this issue to your angels and trust in their love.

Ask the angels to guide you and keep you safe. Your angles have your best interests in mind — trust in their love and wisdom.

You will no doubt feel a little discomfort over the coming days, and perhaps to a lesser extent, over the coming weeks. It may feel as if your emotions are about to explode and that your world has been turned upside down. Persevere. There is nothing to fear — this is the path to being healed.

❧ *Aradia* ❧

It is said that Aradia lived in Italy in the 14th Century. She was known as The Holy Witch because of the love and compassion she held for the Earth and all of humanity. She even had love and compassion for the clergy and the Catholic Church who, at that time, would have had her burnt at the stake if she was caught spreading her message of love or practising her ancient rituals. Her message came to be known as The Gospel of Aradia. It was based on love and respect for Nature, life and all of creation.

Aradia has shown up in your reading today to ask you to look at the belief systems you hold. Question your beliefs and look at them objectively. Try to identify any beliefs that restrict your spirit as well as those that liberate it. We inherit many of our beliefs from our family, our friends and the society we live in. It is time for you to let go of all that no longer serves or supports you. Let go of all beliefs that stem from fear and replace them with love — the endless source of creative energy within you.

This is a good time to study other cultures and diversify your spiritual knowledge and awareness. Look at belief systems both past and present. You may choose to adopt some new beliefs that resonate with you, though there is no need to take on anything new. Simply explore and observe and keep an open mind. Broaden your horizons. You will find that life is a rich and colourful tapestry made of endless truths and viewpoints, and full of tantalizing flavours. Indulge yourself!

❧ *Autumn Leaves* ❧

Embrace the changing seasons of your life and be not afraid. Life is forever changing in accordance with Nature and the Divine will of your soul. Allow Nature and the Universe to guide and heal you. Trust in the flow of life and surrender your will to the will of the Universe. Trust, for the Universe is a loving and benevolent force, of which you are an important part. Just as in Nature, your life is a continuous cycle of changing seasons. Each season holds its own particular beauty and unique vibration.

This period of your life is for letting go of something that has served its purpose and is no longer of any benefit to you. You are being asked to surrender with grace and trust that nothing is ever truly lost, for all exists eternally within the universal life force of creation.

Look at the image on this card and you will see that as the Autumn leaves fall, a beautiful being starts to emerge. This beautiful being heralds a new chapter in your life that is about to unfold. The current events are being divinely orchestrated. All that is required is patience and trust.

The first step is 'Autumn' — letting the old leaves fall. 'Winter' will follow — a dormant period for you to rest and contemplate all you have experienced to date and to give thanks. The flowering of Spring follows Winter, giving birth to a new and exciting chapter in your life.

❧ Blue Angel ❧

Jewels of peace I bestow —
From the sky above,
Are cast oceans of love.

Angels guide and protect humanity. Each angel has a specific purpose, colour and vibration. This card relates to Archangel Michael, whose blue wings surround and protect our entire planet. Regardless of where you are upon this Earth, Michael is surrounding you with his love. He radiates the colour blue and is often referred to as the Blue Angel or the Blue Ray. Look up at the sky and feel the peace and clarity He brings.

To better understand His qualities, imagine for a moment that the sky is red. How would it feel looking up to a red sky each day? A red sky would create a different feeling. Thinking about colour in this way will help you understand the unique qualities each colour has.

Archangel Michael has shown up in your reading to offer you support with an issue or situation that is troubling you at the moment.

Michael will help you release your fear and bring clarity and perspective into your life. Trust— the situation will either be healed, or Michael will help you detach from it, according to the highest good of all concerned. Surrender this issue to Michael and know that it will be taken care of. When you look into the sky, remember, Michael is there, protecting you always. Talk to Michael and share with Him all your concerns and fears. Know He is always listening and remember that no request is too great or too small.

❧ Buddha Nature ❧

Bring your awareness from the external world, to the world within. Breathe in the present and let go of all concern about the past and the future. Remember that eternity exists within each moment. Our past is imprinted in our memory and therefore forms part of the present.

Look back at your past experiences. You will find that it stirs up both pleasant and unhappy memories. We tend to reduce each experience to either good or bad and in the process we rarely see all the blessings in our lives.

Though you may not always see it, everything happens for a reason. Your soul has chosen each of your experiences for its own growth. This can be a challenging concept to embrace, given the pain, suffering and injustice in the world. Why would the soul choose such experiences?

At times, life seems to make no sense and we feel that if there is a God, then He, She or It, must have simply stuffed it all up. We will probably never fully understand the will of the soul just as we will never understand the mind of God.

You have picked the Buddha Nature card in order to release the anxiety and trauma stemming from a past experience and start to live fully in the present. Realise that by focusing on the past or the future you are being robbed of the present. Make a conscious choice to cut all negative ties with the past and to stop worrying about what the future holds.

Bless all your life experiences and release them with love. Accept that there is a higher purpose to everything in life even though we may not understand it. Know that there is a gift to be found in all experiences and with time, this gift will be revealed to you. Reclaim your life by directing all of your precious energy into this moment.

❧ Butterfly Wings ❧

Butterfly wings have shown up in your reading today to mirror the beauty inside you — the sacred beauty that is you.

A deep transformation is taking place in your life. You have managed to reconcile issues from your past and as a result, your true nature is now beginning to emerge.

This card is here to encourage you to continue on your spiritual journey and to continue to be yourself. You have much to offer the world by just being you.

Love is magical, for it has the power to transform all things. The love you hold has the power to touch not only those around you, but the whole world. In becoming aware of your own beauty, you are not only empowering yourself, but you also help to mirror beauty in others.

This card is connected to Nature and the healing power and beauty She radiates. Nowhere is it easier to feel the magic of the Universe at work than in Nature. Nature exudes peace, love and tranquillity that touch the heart. She reflects the love we have inside ourselves.

Regularly set aside some time to surround yourself with Nature. Her magical powers will help reflect the magic within you. The coming weeks and months will bring healing into your life. As your spiritual awareness deepens, so too will the awareness of all that you are, expand and deepen. This will have a magical effect on your life that will be felt not only by you but by all those around you. A time of transformation, of magic and beauty is about to unfold in your life.

Butterflies are a powerful symbol for you at present; symbolic of the transformation that awaits you. Over the coming weeks, take heart every time a butterfly flutters into your field of vision, for it confirms the wondrous progress you are making.

❧ Compassion ❦

You are a jewel.
Even though you may not see it,
All that you consider to be imperfect
Allows greater light to shine through.
Even in darkness you are eternally bright.

Kuan Yin is known in Buddhism as the goddess of compassion and mercy. She views all of life with compassion and has shown up in your reading today to ask you to be compassionate towards yourself.

Kuan Yin asks you to reflect on the many times you have critical thoughts about yourself. Make an effort to replace these negative thoughts with positive and loving ones. Your spirit lives always in perfection, even though from the physical plane you may perceive that you are less than perfect. Perfection exists in all things, even though we may not always see it. All is perfect and all is sacred.

Remember that you are simply spirit clothed in matter in this journey of life. From a spiritual perspective, life is a game and its sole object is for you to remember who you truly are. You are an eternal being and you hold enormous power. Your mind may see imperfection in many things, yet in reality there is no such thing. The mind is bound by logic and judgment and therefore lacks spiritual awareness and compassion. What matters to your spirit is not that you strive to perfect your flaws, but that you accept them and view everything through compassionate eyes. Compassion sees through all veneers and recognizes the beauty in everything. Accept all of who you are and you will begin to see the beauty that surrounds all of life. Be compassionate towards yourself and you will see all the beauty that you are.

❧ *Creativity* ❧

*The power of creation lies not in the
external world, but within.
It exists not in thought,
but in feeling.
Your feelings are the gateway to creation.*

Creativity is a yearning inside your soul; the life
force and fabric of creation. You are a creative being
by nature and the creative power you hold is far
greater than you realise — as great as any artist that
has ever walked this Earth. Your creativity is endless.

You have drawn the Creativity Card today to
unlock the creative power you hold and bring
greater joy and wonder into your life. Creativity
is not restricted to art and music; it can be applied
to every facet of your life — your work, recreation
and relationships. All these things will grow and
transform in ways you never thought possible when
you embrace the creative power of the Universe
that you hold within. The time is right for you to
let go of any fear or apprehension you have
regarding creativity.

Set aside all critical judgment and just be you. Express exactly how you feel without worrying about what others will think. Let go of preconceived ideas and allow your full expression to flow through. Keep a journal in which you can start to express everything that you think and feel. Write down everything that comes to mind. Include all your dreams and wishes... allow your imagination to run wild! It is important that you feel safe to write anything that you wish, without having to worry about whether anyone else will read it, so keep it private.

You may also choose to paint or draw how you feel. Once again, do not think about what you will paint or draw. Just have fun and allow your intuition and feelings to express themselves however they wish.

Every mark you make, even if you think it is just a scribble, is expressing and releasing something. If you choose to work with colour, simply choose the colours you are drawn to, without thinking too much.

You may also choose to share your ideas and feelings with someone you trust. This process will also help you express yourself and overcome your fears. Try not to judge the outcomes of these creative processes. Simply allow yourself to express your inner feelings freely.

Creativity is a feeling, it cannot be thought out, or be limited by trends, or made to fit whatever is currently popular. Creativity is your inner child, the spirit of who you are. It yearns freedom. It is up to you to set it free.

✣ *Dreaming Heart* ✣

Do not lose sight of your purpose,
Know that your efforts are being rewarded.
But do not dwell on this, for your greatest
reward is the love you are helping to create
in the world.

This card is confirmation that because you have been working from your heart, you are having a positive impact on those around you. You are a healer by nature for you hold great love in your heart. This love radiates from you and is spiritually felt by all upon the Earth. It helps to heal our world. Your angels and guides want you to know that your love is invaluable to the Earth and those around you at this time. They understand that you sometimes feel that your work goes unnoticed, at times you may even doubt whether it is having any effect at all. Even though you may not always be able to see the positive effects your love and encouragement have on others, please take heart in the knowing that they do. Each time you offer love to others, be it through a loving gesture, thought or word, you plant the seed of love in that person. They may choose to let the seed lay dormant for a while or to let it sprout — the timing is up to them. Rest assured however, that everything you do has an effect, whether visible or not. Love generates love. Trust dearest one, trust in the love we have for you and in the love you have for others. You will receive some positive feedback in the next few days from someone you unknowingly helped recently. Take this as further positive confirmation of what we have said and remember it next time you start to doubt yourself.

❧ *Dreaming Landscape* ❧

Nature is magic, a wondrous creation forever changing. You have picked this card today to help you remember the importance of spending time in Nature and connecting with its healing qualities. Allow the sunlight and breeze to caress your face. Observe the sense of timelessness that is felt when surrounded by Nature, all in perfect order, all in perfect union. Spend some time alone and allow your mind to be cleared of all thoughts and concerns. Sit in silence and listen to the breeze, feel the trees sway, hear the birds sing and feel the warmth of the sun. Perhaps you have lost your perspective on life, forgotten what is truly important. Remember, you take nothing but your soul with you when you pass from this world, so pay attention to your soul — nurture it, allow yourself to dream and be filled with the magic and healing energy of Nature and the Universe.

❧ Dreaming of You ❧

Life is a journey in which nothing seems to be permanent. Friends and loved ones move through our lives, often leaving a sense of sadness when we part. Life is forever changing. We cannot physically hold on to anything or control the flow of life. We each have our own path with its own challenges and in order to cope with separation from a loved one, we must realise that in reality there is none. The physical body is but a shell that houses our spirit. On a spiritual level, we are always connected to one another. Neither distance nor time can separate that which has been united by love.

This card represents someone that you long to be with again. It is here to remind you that it is only normal that you should miss someone who is dear to you, but to remember that in love, there is no separation. While you may have distanced physically, know this is only an illusion, for the spirit of life is eternal. Those we love live always in our hearts.

❧ Earth Changes ❧

As we begin the new millennium, the energies which have affected and influenced our Earth for the past two thousand years have shifted to make way for the new energies now emerging. The Age of Pisces is over and a new cycle has begun. The long awaited New Age of Aquarius is now with us. Through Aquarius, we will start to change the way we think and feel. The way we each perceive life is already changing and will continue to do so. There is now a giant infusion of love streaming down upon the Earth and swelling out from within its heart, just as love is streaming down upon you and swelling from within your own heart. This influx of love is changing your awareness of life and affecting humanity as a whole.

Dearest one, do not fear the changes occurring in your life right now for all is happening according to the Divine Plan. Do not resist or be afraid of the changes taking place in the world around you, for the current events are simply paving the way for the Golden Age that is about to dawn. Remember above all, that the Earth changes are occurring primarily within your heart and mind and within the hearts and minds of all humanity, and as a result, the Earth is being affected.

Allow the love in your heart to illuminate all darkness. Be positive and bright about the future in the knowing that soon all darkness will be transformed. If there is any confusion, fear, pain or suffering in your life at the moment, remember that it is all part of the transformation process. Your spirit is bringing to the surface all that no longer serves you and all that still remains buried in your heart and memory in order that you may be cleansed and healed. Know that in doing so, your life will be filled with new and beautiful energies that will enable you to fully embrace and be part of the Golden Age of Aquarius.

❧ Earth Song ❧

A forgotten memory lies buried within my heart...
an ocean of scattered feelings, windblown pages
and ancient days spread like autumn leaves
on a grassy field.

Mother Earth is in need of healing. She asks that you pay attention to her needs and spare her a loving thought. In this time of great change, we often forget that it is Mother Earth that feeds, houses and nourishes us. She provides the air we breathe, fuels our cars, supplies the electricity we use, and takes our refuse.

The Earth Song card has shown up in your reading today to remind you of your deep connection to the Earth. The Earth breathes and feels, just like you. At times she sings for joy and at times she cries. She is a reflection of humanity. She is one with you.

You are being asked to think about your relationship with the Earth and the little things you can do in your everyday life to help both yourself and the Earth through the current changes.

The Earth is a conscious entity. Your love will help her regain her balance. In turn, know that the Earth also loves you. Feel and accept her love, for it will nourish your soul. Invoke this great healing power and your life will take on new meaning.

Spend some time in Nature. Meditate on Her beauty and fill yourself with Her gentle and loving vibrations. Keep an open heart and mind as you embark on this new and wondrous phase in your life.

❧ Eternity ❧

It is impossible for the human mind to imagine the vastness of the Universe — it cannot cope with infinite space. The mind will struggle eternally to understand the concept of an ever-expanding Universe. It reasons, "if the Universe is expanding, then there must be something bigger than the Universe itself for it to expand into". The mind is forever trying to contain the concept of infinity into something tangible and comprehensible.

This card is encouraging you to detach from the restrictions of your mind and look at your life from a more universal perspective. If you try to make your life fit entirely into human logic, you are always going to get to a point where it will no longer make any real sense. This is because, just like the Universe, your existence is eternal and infinite. You have no beginning and no end. This present life is but a speck of your eternal being. Trying to make sense of every part of your life is like trying to piece together a jigsaw puzzle while having only a few small pieces of the puzzle in your possession. This is the way it is. It is human nature to strive to work everything out and try to control life. Yet, eternity exists within our spirit, not within our body or mind and therefore the eternal nature of things is not within human reason or understanding.

The message for you at this time in your life is to focus on the spiritual side of life. Observe your thoughts and fears and consciously surrender them to the universal, eternal spirit of life within you. Feel the spirit of Nature and Her changing seasons. Observe how all of Nature is in perfect order, how She accepts all that transpires in the world. Rejoice in the feeling of timelessness that swells within your heart when surrounded by Nature's beauty.

⊰ Floating Memories ⊱

Memories are the recollections of all that has enriched your life, and time is a sequence of events through which life is experienced and memories are created. You are who you are because of your history, and that history is held within your memory both on a conscious and subconscious level.

Through this card, you are being asked to release the judgments you hold of past experiences. Know that past 'failures', 'losses', and pain were serving a purpose in your life. Realise that whether you feel that those experiences were positive or negative, you have grown from each one.

You are here on this Earth to have experiences that deepen your awareness and strengthen your soul. Embrace the past, forgive all that has occurred and liberate yourself. Live fully in the present and remember that you are not the same person you once were, for life is forever changing. Move forward and explore life in whatever way your heart desires.

By drawing this card, your soul wishes to make you aware that a wondrous experience is coming your way. For this new experience to enter your life, you first need to come to terms with and release the past. This card is confirmation that you are ready for this release to occur. All it takes is a conscious desire to do so.

Let go — embrace the present and life will feel new and exciting. You are paving the way to a brilliant future by embracing your past. Our soul chooses what we experience in life and everything has its purpose. There is no need for continual judgment of each episode of your life. There is no need to hold on to feelings of failure or regret. Each experience of your life and your reaction to it has been perfect for you at that time. The important thing is to learn from each experience, find the gift it brings with it and move forward.

❧ Golden Memories ❧

A Fable

A long time ago, a great peace prevailed upon the Earth and love flowed like a golden river, through each heart. The Great Spirit, Mother Nature, shared Her abundance with all and Heaven truly was a place here on Earth.

Slowly, with the passing of time, things began to change. Feelings, which until then had been alien, crept into people's hearts as ego began to appear, splitting and dividing as it does. People began to see each other as separate; they formed separate groups, and began to feel separate from Earth and Nature. Eventually, the beautiful feeling that existed in people's hearts began to fade and the Earth wept with sadness, until one day it wept itself dry. The fertile lands became a desert of windswept dunes. As hearts became barren, so too did the land.

Connection to the Great Spirit was lost.

I remember walking this barren land in a dream. Alone, dressed in crimson robes, with sadness in my heart, I looked out over the distant plains, and watched the last rays of sunlight disappear over the horizon and cast the world into darkness. The dream faded, as a golden era slipped into history.

Perhaps this little story is more than just a fable. Maybe it's a memory we each hold, tucked away in our hearts. A reminder of how wonderful life can be when love becomes our guiding light. It is also the remembrance of how easily the world can change when love no longer prevails. Planet Earth is in the process of major change. We are moving from darkness into light, from fear to love, and from war to peace. Hold the vision of love and peace in your heart, for you will help to manifest these qualities in our world.

This card has appeared in your reading to help ease your fears and concerns about the future of our world. Release your fear and know that all is happening in accordance with the Divine Plan. Visualize peace and love in your meditations and prayers, and have faith, for peace will prevail upon

Earth. Trust — even though at times you cannot make sense of all that is happening. Trust in love, for ultimately it is through love that peace will come about.

All the 'doom and gloom' that exists in our world at present is part of humanity's cleansing. As all the hatred and fear in the world surfaces and is released, it creates opportunities to heal. Fear not, for you are safe. All is held within the eternal embrace of love. We are all part of one Eternal Spirit, which can never be lost or destroyed. All is eternally held in the loving hands of God / Goddess /All That Is. The storm will clear and reveal the light that exists within each heart. You can be of great assistance to those around you at this time by showing faith and remaining positive about the future of our planet. Trust — for all is exactly as it should be.

❧ Healing ❧

The light of creation is the healing power of love —
A light you can turn on any time you wish.
Invoke this sacred power, for you are ready to heal.

Dearest one, I come with love and healing. I reflect the stars that shine eternally bright. You are much greater than you know. You are so much more than this physical existence, for you are eternally linked to the spirit of creation. You and all living things are powerful beyond measure for the essence of creation is within you. This essence is love. It has the power to liberate and heal. You are a Divine being, restricted only by your own beliefs. Any inadequacy you may be feeling is simply due to a lack of love for yourself. Heal yourself through the power of love; the light of spirit forever glowing throughout the Universe. If darkness fills your life know that you can turn on the light at any time. The light switch is within you, dear one. Be in touch with all you truly feel and unlock all that remains hidden in your heart. A good way to do this is through journal writing.

Take some time each day to write down all your thoughts and feelings. Expressing yourself in this way will help activate your healing.

Healing is a process, so be patient. At times it may feel like things are getting worse, however this is part of the healing process. As you start to uncover and release all that you have stored inside, you can often feel emotionally, mentally and/or physically out of balance. Once again, be patient, for things will improve. Trust — for a wondrous and lasting transformation is unfolding in your life.

❧ *Intention* ❧

On an energetic level our world is like a giant fish bowl. Our thoughts are like little fish. When a fish swims, its moving fins create ripples that flow throughout the bowl and are felt by all. In the same way, your thoughts create movement that affects and changes the balance of things around you.

Energetically, we are all connected. We exist within one collective consciousness. Our thoughts, feelings and intentions are living energies. Therefore, each thought and intention you hold creates ripples that energetically affect all upon the Earth. Thoughts, feelings and intentions are the fabric and structure of our world.

This means that we each, individually, have the power to change the world. This power stems not so much from what we try to do, but from the thoughts, feelings and intentions we carry. Remember, that thoughts and intentions are energy. They radiate out into the collective consciousness of our world. Every intention you hold resonates to a particular vibration. Love, joy, hate, fear and so on all have a unique vibrations.

Each of these energies flows out into the world and becomes part of the collective consciousness of that particular thought field or vibration. Loving intentions join with all the love that exists in the world to create more love. Fearful thoughts join with all the fear that exists in the world to create more fear. So, if you want to change the world, you must start with yourself. Only allow positive and loving thoughts about yourself, other people and the world to flourish.

Your intentions and thoughts are the greatest power you hold. Commit yourself to creating more love in our world!

❧ *Lady of the Rose* ❧

Cast in an ocean of stars,
Her reflection fills the galaxy, sky and oceans.

The Lady of the Rose represents purity, innocence and wisdom. She holds mystical powers that are born of these qualities and is here to mirror these qualities, which also exist within you.

We are led to believe that in order to gain knowledge we must study existing formulas, doctrines and beliefs. While study may be a rich and rewarding experience, it is also true that all you need to know is inside you.

Your purity, innocence and wisdom are clouded at the moment as a result of too much formality and theory. You do not need further formal qualifications in order to validate what you wish to do with your life. Do not search externally, for all you wish to know is already inside you. A vast treasure of knowledge and sacred truths exists in the mystical power you hold and it is now time to access this wisdom and claim your power. The Lady of the Rose is here to help you access the endless knowledge you hold in the light of your heart. Here is an exercise that may help you.

Sit quietly and comfortably and let all your thoughts and worldly concerns just drift by. Watch them float away and let go of any expectations you have — simply relax and breathe. The more you can switch off and relax, the easier it will be to connect with your inner self. Knowledge may come through feeling or intuition, or it may come as words that float through your mind. Remember, the secret is to not make this process a struggle; use it as relaxation without attachment to the outcome. Ask the Universe to help you connect to all the knowledge that would best serve you at this time.

⊰ *Lilac Mist* ⊱

Like a million rose petals blown to eternity,
Like light, lost in its own glow.

You may feel that in the past you've blown your chance for happiness or that you have already missed out on something that you yearn for. Lilac Mist has shown up today to remind you that your life is always perfect; you are always at the right place at the right time. Your guides and angels surround you at this very moment — stop and feel their presence. They offer unconditional love and support and ask you to remember that you are an eternal flame, constantly radiating love even though you may not be aware of it.

Stop the internal conflict created by your thoughts and make love your focus. What you perceive to be a setback or failure is the Universe's way of guiding your life to bigger and better things. Much happiness awaits you! The only thing you need to focus on at the moment is yourself.

Dear one, how long has it been since you have truly loved yourself and acknowledged your beauty and special gifts? You are being asked to love yourself and forgive all you consider to be failure. Practice the art of forgiveness daily. Feel the unconditional love your angels and guides have for you. Ask for their help and know that true happiness awaits you. Embrace all without judgment. Make this your focus and watch your life transform. Miracles will manifest in your life when you learn to truly love and accept yourself. There is always a higher purpose to everything that happens or doesn't happen.

Focus on the light inside your heart and
allow it to transform your life.
Your life — present, past and future —
exists in perfect and Divine order.

✤ Lost in Our Own Equations ✤

You may be feeling confused at the moment; perhaps something in your life is beyond your comprehension. Do not waste valuable energy trying to work it all out. Remember that everything in life is constantly changing. Your confusion is simply a result of you not accepting life as it comes. This refusal stems from a fear of that which you cannot control or understand. Look at the history of the world and ask yourself, "what have the countless theories, assumptions and equations that humanity has come up with throughout the ages achieved?" Our world is as confused as ever. Confusion, stress and anxiety have penetrated deep into the human psyche as a result of a need to work everything out.

You need not figure anything out in order to make sense of life. Let go and start to live. Accept life as it is and focus on the light within you. Trust — there is always a higher purpose to everything. The only thing that will help you make sense of your life is love and acceptance. Allow love into your life. Love needs no understanding, but only to be felt.

Within you flows a stream of light — the light of creation. You are forever connected to the source from which all creation stems. Meditate and focus on the beauty inside you. Connect with your heart centre and experience the overwhelming love that exists within you. Tranquillity, peace and clarity will flow into your life as a result.

❧ Lotus Rose ❧

Love floats upon wings of light that glow
upon all creation — the ebb and flow of life,
creating vast oceans of dreams,
as the Eternal Heart reveals all beauty.

This card heralds a time of positive change that is about to unfold in your life — deep and profound changes, which occur at the heart level. As your heart opens, so too does the Universe, bringing new and loving experiences into your life. You may have been hurt or disappointed recently, however, the weeks to come will bring renewal as new friendships and opportunities start to blossom. These new opportunities and friendships will be deeply inspiring and rewarding. They are the result of the love and faith you have shown in the Universe. In opening your heart you have raised your vibration and therefore will begin to attract all that vibrates to love.

Love is a mirror that reflects all that is luminous.

❧ *Love* ❧

*Love is an endless glow that radiates
in all directions.
It is the cosmic fire of passion,
that burns through all darkness
— the eternal I Am.*

Close your eyes and picture the life force within
every living thing on Earth at this moment — every
living soul, every person, animal, bird and fish,
every insect, butterfly, each blade of grass, tree
and flower all swaying to the eternal motion of
creation, the eternal flow of love. Feel the life
force at one with your own. Allow your mind to
merge with the Wind, the Sun, the Moon and the
Stars. Flow with the streams and rivers and merge
with the Ocean, Clouds and Rain.

Hold the vision and feeling of all that exists
within creation, remembering that the life force
that flows through all these things is the same
energy that flows through you. As you breathe so
too do Nature and the Universe. Feel yourself in
unison with all creation.

Whisper "I Am".

I Am — because I exist.
I Am — the Spirit of Life.
I Am — the wind.
I Am — the rain, the Sun, the Moon and the Sky.
I Am — the consciousness within all things.
I Am Love.

You have chosen this card today, to help you refocus on the awesome power of love that you hold within and to help you reconnect to your Divine and Eternal Spirit. The love card is to do with relationships; the relationship you have with yourself, a lover, a friend or your family. It also reminds you of your relationship with all of creation.

Know that only love for yourself and others can truly make you happy. Love is the ultimate creative power, use it in every facet of your life and in every moment of every day. You will find that all your relationships, including the one you have with yourself will transform through love.

❧ *Luna* ❧

Believe in yourself — you are a wonder
of creation.
Wash away all fear — you will discover a
shining star.
Allow all around you to just be —
let go and trust.

Remember — you are an ocean of light.
And 'we' are a reflection of one another.
Remember also the sacred power of Mother Earth,
of Father Sun, the Universe and Stars.

Let there be always a flame in your heart.
May your passion engulf the Earth,
As each new moment, a new star is born —
through an explosion of love.

Let us be in sacred union with one another —
for there is no greater love than this.

Love shines beyond all that is luminous,
Through the merging of our souls, it moves
the ocean's tides.
We are one eternal heart, forever yearning
creation, miracles and magic.

Rest your mind and bathe in my light.
I glitter the night with jewels,
Then at day break, my Sun shines
upon all creation.
As dew drops emerge, they become a river that
flows towards the ocean of infinity.

May the Stars fill your heart,
like the rays of an ancient Sun.

Through the trees, mountains and valleys,
through the immensity of life,
whose circumference is beyond all measure —
you shine eternally bright.

❧ Magic Tree ❧

You are an artist of light and love.
The holder of sacred truths.
You are gifted and blessed.

It is time for you to be more positive about yourself and release the creative power within you. You have the power to transform your life. A great artist, you are able to create through your thoughts, beliefs and intentions. Start to hold only positive thoughts about yourself and be excited about life. You have the power to create happiness, abundance and joy. Positive thoughts and positive affirmations create positive outcomes. Make your intentions clear, for the Universe is always listening and responds to all your words and thoughts.

Use positive affirmations as colours to paint on the canvas of your life. Allow light and colour into each stroke, into each word and thought. Believe in the awesome power of creation as you affirm all you wish to be and create.

Give some thought to all you want for your life; include all your desired qualities. Write these down as affirmations. Affirm to yourself and to the Universe that you have and are all these things right now. Affirm out loud at least once each day with all your heart and soul. This process has tremendous power that stems from the creative power you hold. You can create the life of your dreams.

Affirmation

I am an artist.
I have infinite power to create.
I feel big.
I am worthy of happiness.
I am worthy of love.
I am worthy of abundance.
I am happy... I am love.
I am abundant on all levels.
I create love in my life.

❧ *Meditation* ❧

Sometimes the voice of God is like a whisper
in our hearts. Sometimes it is a roar
within our soul.
In meditation, God speaks.
Sometimes God comes as a breeze, sometimes a
ray of sunshine and at times She comes as
a moonlit night... Listen.

When we pray, we speak to God and in meditation God answers. But who or what is God?

God is creation, the energy that moves the wind or the smile on a child's face. God is the part of you that yearns for love and happiness; the mystery of all we do not understand. God, like love, requires not understanding but feeling. Your feelings transcend the limitations of your mind and create a space for God to enter. What or who God is matters not, all that matters, is how you feel. The meditation card has appeared in your reading today to help you to feel life from a spiritual perspective.

Sit quietly and empty your mind of all thoughts and concerns. Relax your body and bring your awareness to your breath. Gently observe and follow the breath. As you breathe in, feel yourself detach from the external world of your thoughts. Allow your awareness to move to a world of light that exists within you. Be fully aware of your body and fully present within each moment. As you breathe out, release any tension you hold and feel yourself relax as you become one with the universal spirit of creation. There is no separation; the life force that breathes through you, breathes through all of creation.

As you practice the art of meditation, you will discover that the spirit of creation has a voice. This voice can be a feeling that swells inside your heart or a thought that drifts through your mind. It can come as an image or as a stream of light or as midnight blue on a starry night.

❧ Music of the Spheres ❧

Music heals the soul, transcending culture and ideology and bridging the gap so often created by conflicting beliefs. In drawing this card, your soul is asking to be filled with music that inspires you. Immerse yourself within the sound, for it will reconnect you to a part of yourself, which has been long forgotten.

An ancient knowledge exists within you that is beyond verbal description and can only be accessed through the power of sound. It will help to raise your vibration and enable you to discover your hidden talents.

You may be feeling that life has become stagnant and on a subconscious level you have requested help. Your prayers have been heard and answered.

You are about to enter a period of intense spiritual change through which you will rediscover and embrace the many aspects of your nature that have lain dormant for some time. This card is also acknowledgment of the spiritual progress you have made to date. Your angels and guides want you to know that while they understand that your journey has often been difficult and perhaps even painful, the new phase of your life that is about to unfold will be one of wonderment and joy. You have reached a level of consciousness that will easily support you through the coming time, the culmination of which will see you resonating to a higher and finer frequency.

You will become a source of wisdom and inspiration for many who will cross your path simply because of the energy and vibration you hold.

The new energy you are about to access will come simply as a deep inner knowing bringing new perspective to your life. In the future, you may wish to use this energy to help others access the same vibration and knowledge within them. Reiki and other similar healing modalities are an ideal way to work with this energy.

✤ No More Wounds ✤

Love and life entwined, melting into oneness.
Sheltered in one another, yearning to discover
the secrets of Heaven and Earth.

Jesus spoke of love and forgiveness, of compassion, peace and non-judgment, and set an example by showing love and compassion to all. He empowered others by reflecting the light that shines within them. Yet what he preached and practised has since largely been distorted, adulterated and ignored by many who have purported to be his representation on Earth. As a result many of us have come to believe that we are powerless. Global consciousness has been impregnated with denial and shame, which has developed into victimhood. Many of us are often made to feel bad about ourselves. We are led to believe that we are sinful just because we have been born. We are made to feel inadequate and powerless. This mindset is the source of humanity's suffering.

You have drawn this card today because it is time for you to break free from the restrictions caused by such beliefs.

Your life is on the verge of a beautiful transformation, yet in order for this transformation to occur you must first examine your beliefs.

You are worthy of happiness. You deserve to be and have all your heart desires. Honour, respect and love yourself, for in doing so you honour God/Goddess.

You are a Divine Spirit. It is possible for you to replace the negative image of wounds and suffering with the image of joy and happiness. Free and empower yourself by letting go of false and restrictive beliefs. Honour the beautiful being that you are and watch your life transform.

❧ Oceana ❧

Oceana presents you with a gift. She is the balancer of emotions. The gift she brings is one of healing through balance. This healing will help you to better cope with everyday stresses.

You are a sensitive soul and because of this, the world can seem rather harsh at times. You are being asked to imagine the life you truly desire. Start to live your own truth regardless of what others expect of you.

This card is also connected to creativity. You are encouraged to pursue some form of creative expression; explore your creativity and allow it to be expressed imaginatively and emotionally. Through this expression you will discover your future work, which will be emotionally rewarding and enable you to live an imaginative, creative and fulfilling life surrounded by many like-minded friends.

❧ Om ❧

Eternal love moves the Ocean through the spirit of creation. A world of light and eternal sound scattered throughout the heavens, moved by a will beyond its own. The Planets and Stars, entwined within eternity.

If we were to trace creation back to its source it would lead to a single point of light. A tiny point, smaller than we can imagine. Yet, from within that point stems all of creation — the entire Universe. This point of light also exists inside your heart and inside the heart of every living thing. It emanates a sound; a singular note, which resonates the Eternal Truth.

The Om card has appeared in your reading today to remind you of the unlimited power, knowledge and creativity that can be accessed through sound. If you are feeling out of balance and powerless at the moment, it may be because all too often you give your power away. Know that it is not possible for anyone to take your power unless you allow it. You have lost touch with the power within you.

Sit quietly and meditate on the eternal sound emanating from your soul. Feel its vibration flow through all the energy centres in your body. There are seven main energy centres: Crown Centre — on top of your head, Third Eye — the point between your eyebrows, Throat Centre, Heart Centre, Solar Plexus, Sacral Centre and Base Centre — at the bottom of your spine. Focus on each energy centre one at a time. Feel it being healed and balanced by the vibration of the eternal sound. Feel yourself reclaiming your power as you align with the sacred sound of the Universe. You cannot control what others say or how they choose to behave, but you have total control over how you react and what you will allow. Stand strong in your own truth.

Positively affirm and reclaim your power through the vibration of the eternal sound.

⚘ Past Life ⚘

We each hold within our memory cells all our past experiences and memories, and we carry these experiences and memories from each life into the next. At any point, you are the sum total of all your lives' experiences going back to the beginning of time. This influences the way you react to and experience life in this lifetime.

This card is alerting you to the fact that a current issue affecting your life and your relationships stems from a fear you developed in a past life. You have carried this fear within you for eons. Having some understanding of past lives can sometimes help us to make more sense of our present life. The memory and feelings associated with our past lives can be accessed by sitting quietly in meditation and asking our soul and spirit to show us all that may be of help to us at the present time.

You may be shown a glimpse of the past life or lives that have contributed to your current fears and attitudes and this may help you to understand and heal them. All that is required is that you keep an open heart during your meditation and you feel yourself surrounded by light and love at all times. Ask your spirit, your guides and angels to show you only that which will help you dissolve and heal this issue. Before you finish your meditation, imagine all your past experiences transforming and filling with light and love. Bless both past and present and ask that this healing and transformation continue for the days and weeks to come and to continue also while you sleep.

You can access past life experiences in meditation by yourself provided that you trust in the process. However if you prefer, you can seek the assistance of someone who is experienced in this type of work. In choosing someone to help you, simply ask your spirit, guides and angels to attract the appropriate person for you.

❧ *Power* ❧

We fear power because somewhere deep inside we know that we are all-powerful and that we are the masters of our own destiny. We know that we each create our own reality. Therefore, to step into our own power means we are no longer able to blame or feel victimized by others. To step into our power is to take full responsibility for our lives, thoughts and actions. We find this scary, for in owning our own power we must admit to ourselves that we've had a large part to play in the experiences we've had. We have been led to believe that when life doesn't flow as smoothly as we feel it should, we have failed in some way.

To be truly powerful is to love and accept all our seeming imperfections and to work with what we have to the best of our ability at any given moment. True power is to have the courage to just be who you are regardless of what others may think. Above all, to be in your power requires that you speak your truth without judgment or fear of being judged.

You have picked this card because it is time for you to step truly into your own power. Let go of blaming others or blaming the circumstances in your life and take responsibility for your own life. You can create the life your heart desires. Create a brilliant future, by seeing all that you perceive to be past mistakes and setbacks as a necessary part of your growth. Start to see everything in your life as a gift that is here to help you find your truth. The power is within you. There is no need to fear your own power, for true power is not forceful or aggressive, nor is it necessarily 'perfection'. True power is standing in your own truth and taking full responsibility for every moment of your life.

❧ Purity ❧

At the heart of every being dwells the purity of existence. However, our purity is purposely clouded by our soul to enable us to participate in this human drama. We each to some degree have a distorted view on life. The true essence of who we are is clouded by who we think we are. As a newborn baby enters this life it feels only oneness. It does not feel or see itself as separate to the world but as part of it. This feeling of oneness and belonging, that we are born with, stems from the fact that at a soul level, all is one. As your soul incarnates into this physical world, you are aware that you exist individually, but aware also that you are a part of everything else within creation. In the very early stages of life, this feeling of oneness prevails. However this awareness is soon lost. As the duality of the physical world takes hold, oneness becomes a distant memory that we strive to regain for the rest of our lives. It becomes a yearning within us, a strong desire to reconnect with our spirit, which in turn reconnects us to the spirit of all creation. Yet this is where the illusion lies, for in reality we are never separate from creation or from spirit.

This card is here to remind you of the oneness that exists in all things. Perhaps you have been struggling to find your true nature, purpose or mission in life. Remember that the answers to these questions will never be found in the outside world which is an illusion. Your true nature cannot be found through human reason and logic. It can only be discovered through your heart and through your inner spiritual eye which is able to see your life as it is in relation to all of creation. You are therefore being urged to go within. Set aside time each day to meditate and connect with your spiritual-self and know that in doing so, your life will regain the purity which you seek.

❧ Rainbow ❧

A rainbow is the aura of an angel's wings, which shines even in the midst of storms. It lifts the spirit and gives us hope, shining light into our hearts.

Awaken the child within you and remind yourself of the beautiful and simple things in life. By guiding you to this card, the angels are confirming that you are on the right path. They ask you to keep focused on your dreams and to honour your inner child. Follow your heart and do not give up hope, even though you may be experiencing some setbacks. Trust — for all will be revealed soon.

Draw a picture of a rainbow and pin it to your wall. Imagine yourself protected and guided by the angels and ask them to shed light on your path. Sit quietly and meditate, imagine yourself surrounded and infused with beautiful healing colours. The magical energy of the rainbow will help you to keep faith as you pursue your dreams.

❧ Raphael ❧

Soar above the world into the wonder that you are.
You are higher than the mountain tops
and brighter than the Sun.

You are getting too bogged down in everyday issues and this is keeping you from discovering your true path. To some degree you have lost sight of what is really important and lost touch with the childlike innocence that makes life exciting and fun. Remember when the world seemed like a giant playground just waiting to be explored? When life was simple, yet happy?

Archangel Raphael is here to remind you that you are much more than your career, work or study. Lighten up and stop taking life so seriously. Have some fun, play and jump for joy, just for the sake of it. When you leave this Earth you take nothing with you but your soul. Achievements and worldly possessions pale into insignificance as your soul draws back into that overwhelming light from which all creation stems. So, all that matters in life is that you are happy, that you love and are loved. Love and kindness leave a lasting impression that can never be erased. Show some love and kindness towards yourself and allow yourself to have fun. As you start to lighten up, you will come to see your life more clearly. Have fun; explore different interests and avenues for your life, for in doing so, you will discover the things that truly bring you joy.

Whether in your work, study or play, life can be exciting and fun when you follow your heart. Anything is possible! Raphael offers his assistance to help you break out of your current mould and explore all possibilities in a lateral way. Call on his guidance and you will find there are many prospects for your life, which you have not yet given yourself a chance to explore. A whole new world awaits your call!

❧ *Release* ❧

Cutting Negative Ties

Forgiveness and release form the gateway to new experiences and opportunities to discover more of who you are. Often, passing through the gateway can be painful or difficult, especially when someone has hurt you in some way.

No matter how hard you try, the pain seems to resurface time and time again. Just when you thought you had dealt with it and let it go, something happens to trigger the same old feeling.

You have chosen this card because it is time to release yourself from the negative tie you have with someone who has hurt you in the past and who may be continuing to cause you pain and anxiety because you continue to give power to them through your thoughts.

On a conscious level, you may believe that you have already forgiven and released this issue, however on a heartfelt level, you still carry the scar from this wound. Healing is a process which has many layers and you have now reached the final stage.

What is required is for you to realise that you are still energetically connected to the person or issue that is the cause of your pain and that it is possible to detach from this situation.

The first step is to understand why it is so important for you to forgive and release. You are doing this for you and no one else. Also know that in releasing this issue you are not condoning the person's actions or behaviour but rather you are consciously choosing not to be a perpetual victim to those actions. Realise that by holding on to this hurt you are allowing this person or situation to keep hurting you.

When you are ready, you may find it helpful to perform this ritual. It will help you to cut your negative ties with the person or situation that has hurt you, encouraging you to forgive them and release this issue. You can perform this ritual yourself, but you may choose to seek help from a counsellor or practitioner who is experienced in this energy work. There are also many books available on this subject.

Sit comfortably. Close your eyes and imagine the person or situation that you wish detach from. Imagine both you and the other party being surrounded by white light.

Now, invoke the energy and presence of Archangel Michael or, alternatively you may wish to call upon God / Goddess, your angels or your spiritual guides to help you with the process.

Imagine both yourself and the other party being energetically connected to each other by a blue cord of light; this is the negative attachment you wish to sever.

Now, imagine the blue cord being severed by a sword of light held by God / Goddess, an angel or a spirit guide. As the cord is severed, visualize the other party moving away from your life, carried by the hands of God, and feel yourself engulfed and protected by light and love. Give thanks to God / Goddess, the angels and spiritual guides that have helped you with the process.

✤ Rest ✤

Life... an ocean of eternity.
Time... an illusion existing only in the mind.
Cast away all concerns, come rest in eternal light.

You have become so absorbed in the goings on of everyday life that you have forgotten the importance of taking time out to rest. You may be feeling that there's simply not enough time to achieve everything you aim to achieve. Perhaps you feel as though time is running out. Know these feelings are simply an illusion. You have the power to achieve all you want to with ease, provided you stop immersing yourself in material issues and fears. This card is asking you to rest and detach yourself from everyday concerns. Learn to relax and life will be clearer. Everything falls into perspective when you reconnect with your spirit and all that exists inside your heart.

Spirit lives beyond the restrictions of time and space. Your spirit is eternal; it has no fear and vibrates only to love. Rest — allow love's light to heal your fears and anxieties. Let love guide you — it will bring balance to your life.

As your mind is cleared of all stress, anxiety and concern, you create the opening for your spirit to be felt and heard. You will then be able to communicate with your spirit, and reconnect with the truth and purpose of your life.

Keep an open mind and heart. An idea will soon come to you, which will help you greatly. This idea stems from your spirit. It is a blessing from the Universe that will help bring balance and abundance into your life.

The more you detach from everyday concerns the easier things will become. You will soon start to see your life from a higher perspective and you will find that you have adequate time for all in your life, including taking regular time out to rest.

❧ Return to Silence ❧

As you observe the image on this card, feel it reflect the beauty within you. The gracious swirls of love flowing eternally, in perfect union with all. This card has shown up in your reading today to remind you that the true essence of life exists not in the external world but within.

If there is confusion or trouble in your life at this time remember, the clarity you seek will not be found in the outside world.

Confusion is a result of scattered energy, the constant thoughts we emanate as we struggle for answers. Return to the peace and tranquillity that exists within your soul.

The harder we try, the greater confusion we create. Life is not meant to be a struggle, so stop getting caught up in external events and start listening to your inner voice. Meditate — the peace and clarity you seek is within you.

❧ Rose Quartz ❧

As you weave the tapestry of your life,
Allow each stitch to be sewn with love.

True love radiates in every direction without discrimination. It is kind yet seeks no recognition for its kindness. It gives and receives without condition. To truly love is to show compassion towards every living thing, including yourself, which is perhaps the most difficult thing of all. Peace and happiness can only be achieved through love. World peace relies on our individual ability to find love within ourselves.

The Rose Quartz card has shown up in your reading today to encourage you to reflect upon how you feel about yourself and your life. Is there enough love in your life? Do you celebrate and honour who you are in every moment of every day?

The truth is, you are equal to the greatest being that has ever lived. Whether you realise it or not, your power is beyond measure. Your physical body and personality are merely a shell, only a speck of who you are. Deep in your heart, radiant energy and feelings wallow in an ocean of light — this is the real 'you' — the eternal light of your spirit, the timeless, all knowing, eternal love that transcends your physical form.

Your angels ask you, dearest one, to embrace the awesome power, beauty and wisdom that you truly are. Love yourself. Embrace the beauty that lies within you.

❧ *Sacred Mountain* ❧

Within a vast and ancient land filled with myths of The Dreamtime and surrounded by sandy desert exists a glowing monolith of rock known as 'Uluru'.

This card relates to strength of character, which is derived from a compassionate and loving heart. It reflects the inner strength and compassion that you radiate out to all those around you.

Like Uluru, your energy is magnetic and magical. You are a mountain of strength and hope to many people. Your love and wisdom are strong, grounded and down to earth.

Because of this, you will find that many people will be drawn to you, seeking your advice.

Yet, know that the real attraction occurs on an energetic level; little needs to be said, for your energy is such that it has a calming effect on all those who are touched by it. Your honesty, courage and inner beauty is an inspiration to many people. You are indeed a sacred mountain — able to weather the changing seasons of life while always remaining true to your inner nature and wisdom.

❧ The Universe ❧

Come, open the golden doors
And enter the Universe within you.
Eternity exists inside your heart.

Dearest one, be the light that you are and remember that this life is but a dream — don't take it too seriously. Take only your soul with you on your travels. Speak only from your heart and set aside the endless clutter of your mind whose only purpose is to cloud your truth.

Listen to the wind, as it blows through creation. Feel it caress the leaves on the trees. Sway graciously to the rhythm of the Universe. Be one with the eternal flow of Nature, walk with it, rest within its shelter and allow your heart to heal. Nature and the Universe will peel away each layer that no longer serves you. Dwell not in your illusion, which only carries you into darkness, but feel in your heart an eternal glow — the glow of truth. Be at peace with the forever changing seasons and you will not be left dreaming of summer when winter comes. Shed your fears and be one with each season in your life. Graciously accept all that comes and remember that all is the will of the One whose light fills creation. The nature of the Universe is your nature also. Walk not into the darkness of night without the glow of love in your heart. Rest your mind and feel the moon's glow upon you, feel the interconnectedness of all things. Merge with the spirit of Nature for She will help you transcend all obstacles. Be one with all, for all is one. The flame of love burns brightly inside your heart.

Close your eyes and allow your mind to drift back into time, through the ancient mists, to the beginning. The further back you go, the closer you will find yourself to the present, for time is but an illusion, that masks this eternal moment. Be still, for within your solitude you shall discover that ancient lives are but a whisper away, and that all exists within this moment. This card is a blessing from the Universe.

❧ Turquoise Sea ❧

This healing card is connected to your relationships. Perhaps there is a relationship in your life at the moment that is in need of healing. This card is alerting you to the fact that in order for you to heal your relationships with others, you need to first heal the relationship you have with yourself.

Have you been too hard on yourself? Perhaps a part of you feels disappointed that you have not lived up to your own expectations and therefore you feel that others have failed you also.

Our lives are a constant struggle between the intellect and the soul. The soul strives to help us remember that we are perfect just the way we are, it yearns for us to be guided by our feelings and to follow our heart. It wants us to remember that we are love and that we can rely on love to guide us. On the other hand, the intellect constantly strives to control us through fear. It carries a negative voice that whispers, "You are not good enough, not capable..." and so on. It keeps us preoccupied with false concerns and in the process, keeps us from discovering our true nature.

All that is required to heal this issue is to acknowledge your feelings and embrace all that you are. Start to have positive and loving thoughts about yourself. Regularly set aside time to just 'be' without actually 'doing' anything. You do not have to be doing something all the time to be a worthy person. Drop the expectations you have placed on yourself and allow your life to flow.

In healing the relationship you have with yourself, you will also heal your relationships with others. Life is a complex web of relationships, where all is energetically connected. Your relationship with yourself determines what kind of relationships you have with others or with the Earth and Nature. Start to be more kind to yourself, accept all of who you are. You will find that your existing relationships will either heal and blossom or they will come to an end and be replaced by new and rewarding ones.

✂ *Wisdom* ✂

You are a wise and beautiful old soul. This card confirms that you have taken the right course of action or have responded in a just way in a recent matter. Sometimes the best thing for all concerned is to have the strength to say 'no'. Your recent response will serve to empower you and all else involved.

To have wisdom is to stand in your own truth with love and respect in your heart for yourself, all of humanity, the Earth and all living things. Allow yourself to be flexible like the willow that sways with the wind yet remains strongly rooted in the earth. Life is constantly changing within and around you, yet your core essence remains the same. Love and wisdom do not change, they only grow stronger.

Continue to live and respond to all in your life through love and truth, for in doing so, you honour the spirit of all living things.

You have the power to change
our world through love.

Allow yourself to detach from
all negative beliefs and mind sets.

Let go of all that stems from
fear and go forth in light and love.

Toni Carmine Salerno